A WITCH'S WHEEL OF THE YEAR

TAROT OF THE SORCERESS

A WITCH'S WHEEL OF THE YEAR

BÉRENGÈRE DEMONCY

ROCKPOOL

A Rockpool book
PO Box 252
Summer Hill
NSW 2130
Australia

rockpoolpublishing.com
Follow us! **f** **◎** rockpoolpublishing
Tag your images with #rockpoolpublishing

Originally published in 2021 as Le Tarot De La Sorcière,
under ISBN : 978-2-01-714163-1 by Hachette Livre
(Le Lotus et l'Éléphant)

Edited by Lisa Macken

ISBN: 9781922785053

Printed and bound in China
10 9 8 7 6 5 4 3 2 1

CONTENTS

THE TAROT

INTUITION, DIVINATION, CURIOSITY and a need to connect to something greater: any reason to draw tarot cards is legitimate. The tarot will bring answers to your questions and this is where its magic lies, as the cards will always adapt to your expectations.

Is your question legitimate? Yes, it is. If you read cards just for fun you will have trouble drawing interpretations from the imagery, but it will be diverting. If you look to go further to embark on an introspective or divinatory journey your cards will become an alphabet for you.

The tarot consists of 78 cards or arcana:

- 22 Major Arcana cards numbered 0 to 21.
- 56 Minor Arcana cards divided into four suits (or colours) traditionally called Swords, Cups, Wands and Coins. Each suit includes 10 cards numbered from 1 through to 10 as well as four court cards: Page, Queen, King and Knight.

The Major Arcana cards refer to the great movements of life and intention while the Minor Arcana cards represent practical aspects of life:

- ✸ Swords symbolise the mind: intellect and spirituality
- ✸ Cups correspond to our emotions
- ✸ Wands refer to creativity and sexuality
- ✸ Coins represent the material aspects of our lives: our bodies, money and work.

In the *Tarot of the Sorceress* the four traditional suits are replaced by their respective elements of air, water, fire and earth (see the section 'Why a sorceress's tarot?'). In any tarot Swords correspond to the element of air, Cups to water, Wands to fire and Coins to earth.

The tarot I have imagined draws its inspiration from two distinct traditions: the Marseille Tarot and the Rider-Waite Tarot. In my readings I combine both traditions to create my own practice, and by following that personal pattern I created this tarot. This booklet is completely infused with that combination as well as with my own tradition. However, this tarot can absolutely be used as a Marseille Tarot or a Rider-Waite Tarot or be applied to your own personal tradition if you have one. Another magic aspect of this tarot is that you can own it, sometimes to extremes.

The *Tarot of the Sorceress* includes these elements from the Rider-Waite tradition:

- The imagery is very illustrated and easy to interpret, even with regard to the Minor Arcana.
- The meanings of the Minor Arcana cards are very practical and are grounded in reality.

It also includes these elements from the Marseille Tarot tradition:

- The Knight follows the King, as presented in Alejandro Jodorowsky's book *The Way of Tarot*. This suggests that the Knight is a messenger of the King and therefore moves towards the next suit of cards.
- The numerology preserves the passive/active aspect of the cards (see the section 'Numerology').
- The names, numbers and elements of imagery follow the Marseille tradition.

The interpretations of the cards may differ from your usual tarot if you have one.

WHY A SORCERESS'S TAROT?

I CREATED THE TAROT OF THE SORCERESS based on the wheel of the year, drawing my inspiration from seasonal pagan spirituality. This tarot therefore revolves around seasons and festivals and the sabbats that pace them throughout the year. It is more broadly built as if it were a full participant in the creation of rituals around the four elements of air, water, fire and earth. The Major Arcana cards embrace these great movements of the wheel of the year and the figures of a pagan spirituality.

The Minor Arcana cards are like tools in the service of the Major Arcana, depicting sabbats, seasons, moon cycles, sacred figures, constellations, planets, crystals and plants. Each element has its own force, but together the cards take on a different symbol. Each suit includes:

- ✸ an element
- ✸ a time of day
- ✸ a sense
- ✸ a lunar phase

- ❀ a candle
- ❀ a crystal
- ❀ a herb
- ❀ a flower
- ❀ a magical tool
- ❀ a planet
- ❀ an incense
- ❀ an animal
- ❀ an allegory
- ❀ constellations.

This tarot was created in this way so that anyone can connect with it and use it in their own personal way in a reading, and also by breathing a special intention into an important card or even using it as a pocket altar. I invite you to discover the subtleties of the tarot for yourself and to invest it with your own intentions, feelings, messages and intuitions. Of course, this particular tarot deck does not in any way change the traditional meanings of the Major Arcana and Minor Arcana, instead simply involving multiple levels of reading to which you should feel free to add your own.

NUMEROLOGY IN THE TAROT IS

just as important as all the other elements in the cards. Numbers have something to tell you: they can help you understand a card that may sometimes seem out of place in a spread.

Even numbers are passive and connote a form of inertia such as rest, waiting, contemplation, the past or blockages. Odd numbers suggest movement: moving forwards, sometimes unsteadily and sometimes in order to move on to something else.

The meanings of numbers in the tarot are as follows:

- ❀ one: everything is possible
- ❀ two: duo, a constructive or fruitless relationship
- ❀ three: uncertain, adolescent, enthusiastic/destructive movement
- ❀ four: stability
- ❀ five: something gone awry
- ❀ six: renewed stability, a time of feeling good
- ❀ seven: doubt
- ❀ eight: perfection, a deadline or ending
- ❀ nine: looking further out, moving on to something else

- ✹ ten: being ready for what comes next, making decisions
- ✹ Page: hesitation
- ✹ Queen: grounding in the element
- ✹ King: confidence, completion
- ✹ Knight: a message, moving on to what comes next.

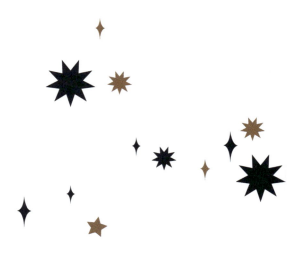

I TEND TO SEE THE TAROT AS AN alphabet: although the letters all look alike, depending on the way you assemble them they form a multitude of languages that have no relation to each other. Find your own language in your tarot cards.

The meanings of the cards are like a compass to define your own language. At first you may need to stick closely to the interpretations in the booklet, but with experience and practice in readings the meanings will connect with your mind, imagination, life experience and way of thinking just as a novel may be adapted instead of translated literally.

What is interesting about the Rider-Waite tradition I have drawn inspiration from is the illustrations on each card. Each element of artwork, each figure, tells a story in this booklet that will put you on the track of the card's meaning without necessarily having to learn that meaning. You may also find yourself imagining your own stories through the imagery, which will mean that you are on your way to owning your tarot. The booklet also includes a short description for each card.

KEY WORDS

Each Major Arcana and Minor Arcana card includes an interpretation that stems from a specific tradition, which is what is indicated with the key words. Even if a card's story helps you understand that card, the key words are good basic material to assist with its interpretation. They will be useful in your learning process if you are a beginner in tarot reading.

THE CARDS' STORIES

The description that follows the key words tells you the story of a card: what it represents, how it relates to the theme and how to understand its symbols. The story also refines the elements of interpretation, which can be useful with complex cards. Part of the symbolism of each card is left to your own interpretation in order to reinforce your intuition, which you should implicitly trust in.

REVERSED CARD MEANINGS

A tarot deck can take into account the fact that a card can be drawn upright or upside down. When a card is drawn upside down its meaning is generally considered to be reversed, which is why reverse key words have been included. For example, the Ace of Fire can represent a new creative project, but if it is drawn upside down you may conclude there is a creative blockage somewhere, a delay in a project or a missed opportunity.

The word 'reverse' rather than 'contrary' or 'negative' is used because there is no obligation to take into account the fact that a card has been drawn upside down. It can add a layer of difficulty in interpreting the cards when you are just starting out, in which case you can just turn the cards the right way up as you draw them from your spread so they are all upright. Cards are interpreted depending on the question asked, and sometimes our intuition tells us that a reverse interpretation corresponds best to the spread. Also, reverse meanings aren't necessarily negative because some cards don't have a positive meaning. In such cases the reverse can be a message of hope.

Feel free or not to take into account the fact that some cards appear upside down. The next section on card spreads provides further information as to why it can be interesting to take reverse meanings into account in a reading.

CARD SPREADS

I never put my cards in order but you can do it for pleasure, plus you can put all of the cards the right way up from time to time. Whatever you decide to do, find a routine that makes it easy for you to:

🏵 Shuffle your deck of cards as if you were playing a usual card game, by mixing the cards up on a table or other surface: you decide.

🏵 Ask your deck a question. I always ask my question in my head as I shuffle the cards a set number of times.

🏵 Select cards for your spread. I like to draw the first cards at the top of the pack after having cut it once, but if you like you can spread the deck out and draw cards randomly. Try a few different ways of drawing cards and choose the one that works best for you. The same goes for cutting or not cutting the deck after shuffling.

Ideally, choose which spread you would like to use before drawing cards. It is up to you to create your own rules with your deck. The more you use it the more you will own it and be comfortable with it.

REVERSED CARDS

Don't put the cards the right way up just to have a positive spread. Bear in mind that the basic meaning of some cards is negative so don't push them away, as sometimes a negative meaning is what the card is actually telling you.

As previously mentioned you can choose to take into account or not the fact that some cards appear upside down when drawn. If you do not take reversed cards into account try not to deny the negative meaning of some cards; they appear to you in order to teach you something that you do not want to know or accept. The tarot is there to take you out of your comfort zone, so do accept the card's message when you feel that the reverse meaning is the one that should be applied.

The reverse meanings of the Minor Arcana cards are presented in the booklet, as in the Rider-Waite tradition. However, the reverse meanings of the Major Arcana cards are not indicated as they are more complex and you will have to learn to discern them on your own. Sometimes Major Arcana cards have such a global signification that drawing them upright or upside down makes no great difference. Refer to the patterns made by the cards.

In the *Tarot of the Sorceress,* as in other oracles of this type, the cards' illustrations give indications as to meaning and tell a story. However, the illustrations also tell a story beyond the cards themselves. When you create a spread the cards are laid down beside, above or below each other, at an angle, a little away from each other and so on. Look at each card individually but also try to discern any global patterns: do any cards seem to respond to each other? Are any figures' faces turned towards each other? Does a figure give an impression of falling into the landscape of another card? You can take all these collateral stories into account to complete your interpretation.

This is where it would be interesting to leave cards drawn upside down as they are – patterns will be different according to whether cards are upright or reversed. Pay attention to these patterns.

ONE-CARD SPREAD

Justice

A single card can bring an answer to an introspective or divinatory question such as 'What should I work on this month to feel better?' If you draw the Justice card it means you need to bring balance back into your life. Go over things with a pragmatic eye: weigh the pros and cons and restore balance in your relationships, diet and lifestyle.

If the message imparted by the card isn't clear enough draw a second card for additional information and let that further information give you your answer. There is no need to draw a further five or ten cards, especially if you are a beginner.

THREE-CARD SPREAD

Traditionally a three-card spread represents the past/present/future; however, you can also read it as a sentence using your gradually emerging alphabet. Like the one-card spread, the three cards you draw will offer an answer to your question or to the question of your interlocutor, but in three steps. The past/present/future pattern emerges often, but the cards frequently interact together to create a unique message. You can again take into account the interaction between the cards' illustrations. For example, with the question 'What should I work on this month to feel better?' your draw is:

Four of Water + The Star + Eight of Air

As a Major Arcana card The Star represents an important aspect of your life right now and indicates you need to find your path or get started on a project that particularly matters to you, and you need to think about it and make it grow inside you. This card is framed by two other cards as if to make it safe. Two possible avenues are open to you to secure that important momentum in your life. The Four of Water indicates a time of calm, of rest or even of retreat from the world. The Eight of Air, to all appearances a negative card imposing limits, can simply be a suggestion to secure a mental and/or physical space for yourself in order to think about the direction you want to take or how to set up a project or path before showing it to the world, and to define the boundaries of that personal space with regard to the people around you or in your own mind and make space and time for everything.

I like the three-card spread because it is simple and often brings insightful answers without muddling my mind with too much detail such as external influences or future possibilities. This spread really focuses on the question.

In this traditional spread, as with many other spreads, the cards correspond to aspects of a question. The cross spread proposes to answer your question in this way:

Card 1: represents you
Card 2: the issue at hand
Card 3: past events
Card 4: the outcome

After asking the question 'What should I work on this month to feel better?' your draw is:

Queen of Fire

Four of Water

The Moon

Five of Fire

The card that represents you is the Four of Water: you are in a period of stagnation, in mid-water, no longer really knowing if your reflection is the reality or not. You are lost. A negative card, the Five of Fire suggests how you have generally let yourself go. The passion of the Queen of Fire, which might prove to be suffocating, represents what has generated this state of depression: a toxic relationship, a time-consuming personal project or your tendency to smother others, which in the end caused them to reject you or in which you no longer recognise yourself. The Moon invites you to take some introspective personal time, during which you will have to dig deep to find what you can't admit to yourself. You need to face reality and stop living in a world of illusion.

Through this example you can see how the cross spread also reveals a past/present/future pattern. It is very simple to follow if you are a beginner or if you still like to refer to the booklet to interpret the cards.

This is a spread of my own invention to accompany this tarot. In it each card corresponds to an aspect of the question, and the spread as a whole will guide you in your questioning. Lay the cards down starting with the bottom of the pyramid and work your way upwards in your order of reading.

Card 1: what you hope for
Card 2: what must be eliminated
Card 3: what must be taken into account
Cards 4 and 5: actions to undertake the first three points
Card 6: external guidance

After asking the question 'What should I work on this month to feel better?' your draw is:

Temperance

Seven of Air

Five of Earth

The Emperor

Ace of Water

The Empress

These cards indicate the following.

What is hoped for: The Emperor invites you to move on to the next step, to give shape to your ideas and feel powerful enough to bring your projects to life with strength and determination.

What must be eliminated: the Ace of Water shows that you have been indulging in your own emotions, in overflow or in a lack of emotional control. It is time to see the world through other prisms. By multiplying points of view you will broaden your outlook and, in doing so, expand your field of possible reactions and solutions.

What must be taken into account: The Empress highlights your need to create and grant importance in your inner world, and also what brings you closer to your innermost being. Perhaps it is time to listen to your inner child and let them act as they will without worrying about the consequences.

Actions to undertake the first three points: the Seven of Air invites you to sort through things in your life and determine what is toxic or pulls you down in order to find the solutions that need to be applied. If you want to create or bring your projects to life, rid yourself of what keeps you nailed to the ground out of fear or influence – of the people around you or of ingrained patterns. This can take a while because it is deep work that requires you to lift a few veils and face the truth. The Five of Earth invites you to be patient, which echoes the Seven of Air. When you look to change things or transform yourself there will always be a period of deterioration before improvement starts to manifest. Find a way to keep your goal well in mind and accept the adversity on your path, as you will learn from it.

External guidance: don't shut yourself away in your shell to attain your goals or, contrarily, dive into action at the expense of your physical or mental health. Temperance indicates you are going to have to find some balance in your process of coming and going between your inner world, your need for change and the realisation of your projects or your relationships with others.

THE MAJOR ARCANA

THE FOOL

0

The sorceress embarks on a spiritual path

travel, evolution, detachment, exploration, marginality, journeying, fragility, freedom

THE FOOL REPRESENTS THE STARTING point of a sorceress's journey. Who is she? Is she embarking on her spiritual path and mounting her broom for the first time or is she already on a journey that was begun long before? One thing is sure: she is moving and she still has many things to explore and discover. She has chosen to be a sorceress and live marginally, and to define herself in this way. In doing so she knows she will have to struggle against preconceived notions but that her path will be filled with magic, enchantment and occasional mistakes that will help her grow. She is accompanied by her symbols of the four elements – her broom, black cat and mortar and pestle for her potions – and she might have inherited these from Baba Yaga. She is The Fool, and she is getting ready to visit with the Major Arcana of the tarot with all the innocence of a new adventurer or the excitement of renewing an adventure at her own pace and in her own way. She is unique.

Traditional key words: travel, searching, strangeness, freedom, chaos, madness, detachment, lack of judgement

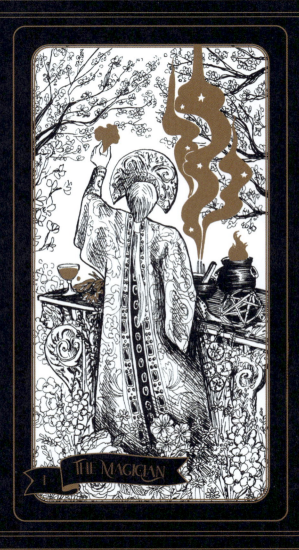

THE MAGICIAN

THE MAGICIAN

Spring

starting out, tools, potential, skills

THE MAGICIAN IS PREPARING AN altar for spring, the season of new beginnings, of blooming nature's potential and of preparation.

Everything is at hand to make a start: magical tools and the skills of the sorceress. The ritual must be carried out and room must be made for budding. The elements of air, water, fire and earth are present again, here on the altar with incense, a cup, a cauldron and herbs. The Magician is also surrounded by the messengers of spring: cherry blossoms, peonies, cinquefoil, meadowsweet, daisies, the first hollyhocks and poppies.

Expressing a potential, The Magician is preparing the tools and is in an energy of action, evolving the idea of a creation, something practical to bring to life. This figure of potentiality can sometimes indulge in showing off or creating magical illusion.

Traditional key words: cleverness, new beginnings, skill, youth, potentiality, bringing to life, disciple, talent, cheating, mischief

KEY WORDS   observation, study, passiveness, intuition, secrets

THE HIGH PRIESTESS HOLDS THE secrets of a deep study of which she has everything to teach you. What does her book contain? Why does she want to keep the secret? Only her hands appear, all the better it seems to conceal her identity or to hide what she is. There is a mystery to discover here and many things to be learned. What matters is what is said or written, not who says or writes it. The High Priestess represents a passive, dedicated time. Her hands represent the connection between the seen and the unseen, as if calling upon intuition to divine what is hidden. This card invites you to listen to that intuition, to the intangible, and to take the time to learn what must be learned.

Traditional key words: faith, knowledge, patience, purity, solitude, silence, rigour, gestation, virginity, cold, resignation

THE HIGH PRIESTESS

THE EMPRESS

III

THE EMPRESS

Beltane

developing ideas in your mind, conception, creativity

HE EMPRESS IS DANCING FOR the Beltane sabbat. It is spring, hearts are having fun and everyone is bringing their personal colour to the maypole. Only one of these women is The Empress but the little people are the symbol of the inner riches of all women, as varied as they are excited. Dazzling and pregnant, The Empress moves among the flowering symbols of a promising spring, the symbols of Beltane and celebration: violets, marigolds, buttercups, oak, elder, rowan tree, hazel bush, hawthorn, birch, juniper and pine. The veil between worlds is thin indeed at Beltane, and it leaves the door open to intuition, inspiration, creativity, desire for life and wishes. The Empress invites you to create, to develop ideas in your mind. She is the passionate impulse from your belly and your flamboyant youth.

Traditional key words: fertility, creativity, learning, seduction, desire, power, excitement, nature, elegance, abundance, harvest, beauty, blossoming, creative brilliance

THE EMPEROR

IIII

Litha

bringing to life, crystallisation, new projects, confidence, wisdom

THE EMPEROR IS A CARD OF launching new projects, bringing to life what was created in The Empress's womb. His determined forward movement symbolises how your ideas and creativity are coming to life. The Emperor is also a card of power, shining and benevolent and even paternalistic.

Here The Emperor represents the sun at its zenith. At Litha, the summer solstice, we celebrate the first harvests and the longest day of the year. The sun becomes the benevolent father who warms and protects you and enables you to eat in the long winter months in its absence. The Emperor is surrounded by multiple symbols of the sun in many cultures: the four-petal flower of Kinich Ahau, the rays of Amaterasu, the serpent of Re and the ideogram of Shamash, among others. Confidence, protection and motivation are the feelings that accompany this bright, powerful card.

Traditional key words: stability, domination, power, responsibility, rationalism, solidity, order, strength, paternity, mastering the material world

THE EMPEROR

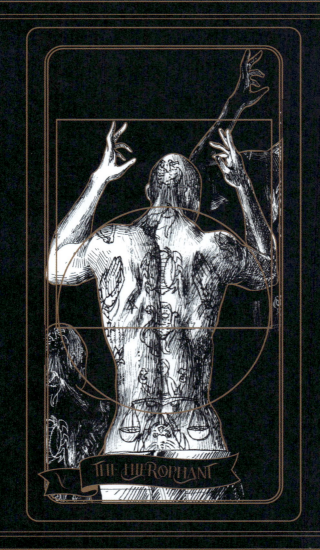

THE HIEROPHANT

THE HIEROPHANT

Sacred masculine

KEY WORDS   deepening, values, orientation

THE HIEROPHANT, A CARD OF orientation and values, is also the masculine aspect of spirituality based on the duality and complementarity of the feminine and the masculine, which are always mingled in the gifts of nature. Here The Hierophant is represented by the sacred masculine. Reaching towards the sky, he evolves and shows you the way or pushes you to find your own way in accordance with your personal values. The sacred masculine has a multiple, multifaceted nature, and it invites you to explore more deeply the parts of your life or your question that are probably a little too static. The sacred masculine requires you to always be aligned with its values in order to move forward.

A bridge between earth and sky, The Hierophant is grounded in the most trivial thing nature has given him – his body – in order to express his intangible will and spirituality.

Traditional key words: wisdom, mediator, faith, teaching, spirituality, guide, power, spiritual ascent

Rhodocrosite, garnet and pink quartz

KEY WORDS **crossroads, choices, decisions, wishes**

THE LOVERS IS A CARD OF LIFE crossroads, decision-making and choices. It indicates the moment when you begin to imagine what you would really like and look further ahead in your life.

This moment is symbolised by the connection between the new moon, representing new starts, the new things you contemplate and the sun, the light and the sky you want to attain. You begin to look higher, to aim at what you love and brings you joy. The three crystals represent the three entities, both similar in their characterisation and dissimilar in their composition and virtues, that are the elements of your life path stretching from the new moon to the sun. They can be pleasant or difficult, and you encounter them when you find yourself at a life crossroads.

The rhodocrosite, at the bottom, is used to heal sentimental wounds and restore harmony between the body and mind. The garnet, in the middle, pushes away obstacles on your path and gives you the strength to face your problems. The pink quartz, at the top, is the crystal

of self-love, peace and balance. These stones pave the way towards a fully realised love, desire or wish.

Life paths are symbolised by the elm boughs branching outwards. Elm bark is used to attract love and protection, and the elm tree outlines plural paths. The branches in the picture represent all the possibilities your mind can imagine and that life can offer you. All you have to do is choose.

Traditional key words: emotional life, union, heart, choices, ambiguity, trio, doing what you love, following your own path

VII THE CHARIOT
Summer

KEY WORDS progress, control, autonomy, independence

THE CHARIOT IS THE CARD of mad dashes forward. He/she is powerful and possesses the energy of success, of those whom nothing can stop. Like summer, The Chariot flies by on the wings of nature's blessings during that season. Joyful and carefree, he/she flits and flies among

VII THE CHARIOT

the chamomile, heliotrope, lavender, poppies, butterflies, birds and bees. He/she consists of all that makes summer a gentle, motivating kind of warmth, giving you the feeling that nothing ever ends – be it the summer days, time, the sun or summer energy. Short days and darkness are still far away. You can only see your progress, your wishes and movement.

The Chariot can squash other cards by being excessive or not knowing when to stop. It can indicate great independence of action and an iron will. The Chariot can sometimes be boastful, carried away by his/her intoxicating assets, or can project a controlled personal image instead of showing his/her true nature.

Traditional key words: action out in the world, lover, triumph, ease, conquest, dominating, warrior, performance, boastful

VIII

JUSTICE

Sacred feminine

KEY WORDS

normalisation, balance, rules, the law

THE JUSTICE CARD CALLS FOR

balance or the restoration of balance, cutting through and separating what needs to be sorted. Through its asymmetry it is also an invitation to bring greater clarity, stability and therefore balance to things.

Justice is like a set of scales, represented here by its two blossoming sleeves. The first is made up of chamomile, daisies, Indian marigolds, primroses, St John's wort, heliotrope, bellflowers and cinquefoil, all soft, spring-like and blooming. The other sleeve is covered in holly, ivy, chestnut burrs and thorny dry yew and brambles, representing the difficulties encountered in the dark and cold of winter when resources are lacking.

The two bundles are almost symmetrical, forming a balance of choices, obvious divergences and differing results. Balance is not always found in light or darkness; it grows between both worlds. Justice does not invite you to choose one or the other but to embrace both, to find a happy medium and open your eyes to what seems complicated as well as what really makes up the true nature of life.

Justice is alone in the blackness of night, because it is during that dark time that nothing is obvious or clear and that each thought and decision is devoured by doubt. Its sword is not at the centre of the picture because it invites you to cut through, to find your personal balance instead of conforming to the norm. Justice draws that imperfect, human delimitation on the ground and represents your choice.

This card can also evoke the need to do justice for yourself or others or the law, the state or the administration. However, it may be interesting to look for what else it wants to tell you beyond the obvious.

Traditional key words: balance, perfection, cutting through, value, judgement, cheating, authorisation, prohibiting, balancing

VIII · JUSTICE

VIIII · THE HERMIT

THE HERMIT

Tibetan bowl

VIIII

KEY WORDS — time, searching, solitude, ripening, remedy

THE HERMIT CARD CALLS FOR meditation, taking a step back or accepting a time of immobility or a blockage that you're subjected to that isn't of your own making. This break in your life is to help you move forward more profitably later on, if you use this time to discern where the light that will guide you is. It can foreshadow a dark period in your life because you can't always see the light on your path.

The meditation time indicated by The Hermit, the monk, is represented by the Tibetan bowl, a meditation tool connecting the physical world and the realm of spirit, of what cannot be put into words. This connection is symbolised by the haunting sound of the bowl, guiding and enabling you to move away and then come back to yourself like Ariadne's thread. The hands form a gesture turned towards meditation – the energy flowing between the thumb and forefinger – with two mudras of concentration and reception: at the bottom the jnana mudra is turned towards the universe, and at the top the chin mudra is turned towards the inner being. The meditation here searches for connection, looking to form a whole while remaining entirely focused on being out of the world.

The two parts of the card are symmetrical: the idea is to form a whole between the universe and the self, to find your own light or your own guide. All of these elements are grouped at the centre of the card in the flower of life, the ultimate goal of this retreat from the world.

Traditional key words: crisis, passage, wisdom, letting go, experience, poverty, asceticism, illumination, moving back, age, silence

X

WHEEL OF FORTUNE

Lughnasadh

KEY WORDS — movement, surprise, opportunity, luck

THE WHEEL OF FORTUNE IS an enigmatic card in the true sense of the word because it raises questions without bringing any answers. It can be a symbol of unexpected luck, of a timely opportunity or, when drawn upside down or depending on the other cards in the reading, of a change in fortune. It generally portends good news but also inexorable change, because nothing is permanent. Everything evolves constantly – the world, events, others, yourself – whether physically or mentally, which means that although the wheel shines brightly in times of harvest such as depicted here, decorated with the symbols of Lughnasadh – wheat, apple blossoms, acacia and myrtle – it can also mean that these rays of sunshine are the last before the first chills of autumn and winter. The Wheel of Fortune indicates it is time to celebrate and be joyful or, conversely, to prepare for tougher times.

Traditional key words: beginning or end of a cycle, fortune, blockages, revival, enigma, solution, impermanence, change, eternal return, heart/body/spirit

WHEEL OF FORTUNE

XI · STRENGTH

XI

STRENGTH

Mabon

KEY WORDS realisation, taming, energy, connection, destiny

STRENGTH HAS TURNED THE Wheel of Fortune and prevailed over what cannot be controlled. It is your inner force, that which positions you in your self-esteem and self-confidence and enables you to tame the world around you and the hurdles that seem so difficult to overcome. It's represented by the autumn equinox, a time to strengthen yourself before winter and fortify your spirit in the face of life's vicissitudes while remaining aware of your own riches. This wealth is external – final harvests, autumn fruits, chrysanthemums, grapevines and abundance before winter – but is also inside you in your qualities, skills, wishes, desires and projects for the future. These things all strengthen you and enable you to project the necessary energy to find your place in the world, your own humble, true, luminous importance.

Traditional key words: new energy, animality, creativity, depth, puberty, action, feeling, force, communication

THE HANGED MAN

Autumn

KEY WORDS   immobilisation, selflessness, change in point of view, transcendence, taking a step back

THE HANGED MAN SEEMS TO BE a prisoner, immobilised by an external element although appearances can be deceiving. He is always voluntarily immobilised or at least is so in order to be able to break free from his bonds on his own. The Hanged Man has created these bonds to force himself to stop and take a welcome break at this time in his life or to stay in this position, upside down in the world, in order to change his point of view on it. The Hanged Man is often an invitation to broaden your view on things, to change perspective in order to examine a problem.

Here the Hanged Man is in the middle of autumn, symbolising his decision to lead an ascetic life turned towards his inner world, towards this self-dedicated time. Autumn isn't all dead leaves; it also brings beautiful things to nature and to the table such as flamboyant colours and delicious foods. Autumn is like The Hanged Man: in transition and open to the best that asceticism and abundance have to offer. This card can also represent a

THE HANGED MAN

period of suspended time, a break or a period in your life that may seem long but can be an opportunity to explore your inner wealth or what you don't usually see in terms of external riches within your grasp.

Traditional key words: stop, meditation, giving of yourself, sacrifice, not choosing, gestation, depth, inversion, waiting, rest

XIII
Samhain

KEY WORDS

brutal transformation, elimination, mourning

THE CARD THAT HAS NO NAME is a card of brutal, boundless transformation that aims to clear the slate of what already exists and remove all that is toxic in your life. This card, sometimes also called 'Death', is the fruit not of an external entity but of your own thinking, your own thread of life decisions. This transformation has meaning at this time in your life, and it can be so brutal as to cause collateral damage if no other card in your reading seems to put an end to this complete elimination.

This moment between what came before and what will come after is highlighted by the festival of Samhain, during which the veil between worlds is at its finest and when death comes to mingle with life. Beings from the other side come to pull the living into a dance about which they do not know the outcome. Nights become longer and start to conceal everything you were once sure of, drawing a veil over all your certainties.

Traditional key words: deep transformation, revolution, mutation, change, anger, cleansing, harvest, elimination, destruction, speed

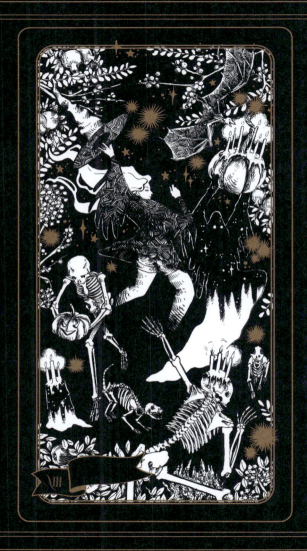

VIII

XIII TEMPERANCE

XIIII — TEMPERANCE

Yule

KEY WORDS   **rebirth, communication, alternation**

EMPERANCE IS A CARD OF moderation, communication, alternation and communicating vessels. It can also represent a guardian angel, the benevolent protection that invites you to show moderation and reflection and elevation of your mind.

Temperance is surrounded by many candles, lights in the heart of darkness, and other references to Yule. Ivy protects the home, while holly symbolises renewal with the reappearance of sunlight and lengthening days. Blessed thistle calls for a purification of the home, and frankincense brings balance in complete harmony with Temperance.

With his/her light and alternation Temperance forges a connection between Samhain, a night of otherworldly creatures, and The Devil card, which represents an essentially inner, hidden world. He/she is a bridge, a path opened both ways that enables round trips and rebalancing. He/she can invite you to explore your own shadows and light, weigh the pros and cons or listen to your intuition without forgetting the voice of reason.

Yule is the shortest day of the year. It is the winter solstice, a festival in which we celebrate the imminent return of the sun. Temperance symbolises all the hope of the shortest day and longest night and the way towards the equinox, the perfect balance. Yule is also a sign of gathering with your loved ones with gifts, love and communication.

Traditional key words: guardian angel, protection, circulation, healing, mingling, harmony, benevolence, prudence, balance

Chakras

KEY WORDS

pleasure, enchantment, vitality, creativity, sexuality, deep desires, shadows

IN OUR COLLECTIVE IMAGINATION

The devil connotes vice or evil, what should be kept hidden deep inside because it is too terrible to be shown to the outside world. In the tarot The Devil has a much more nuanced and deeper meaning than that. You can interpret it prosaically if you wish, but if you do so you will doubtless miss its true essence.

The Devil is the fire burning inside you that motivates you intrinsically and therefore personally, enabling you to start moving so you may attain your goals. He/she is primitive, relentless passion that connects your body together and gives meaning to its existence. In a word, he/she represents what is in your guts. The Devil is neither masculine nor feminine but encompasses both in all that makes up your innermost being beyond gender, appearance, morality and the varnish of education. He/she is your true being with all the qualities and faults that make up its personality.

The card depicts the devil with the seven main chakras, which enable vital energy to flow continuously throughout your body to give it life and united energy. This also shows a form of imperfection because, although the chakras do need to be balanced, perfection is divine and cannot be attained by humans. Is balance perfection? What is your balance? The Devil represents the raw expression of your humanity. This card therefore invites you to shake up your shadows, your darknesses, and explore your deep motivations and identify your inner fire, especially if that fire has been smothered by years of living and a will to conform to an outside mould.

Traditional key words: unconscious forces, passion, creativity, desire, temptation, bonds, depth, darkness, fear, prohibition, taboo, sensuality, impulses

THE DEVIL

XVI THE TOWER

momentum, emergence, challenge, deconstruction/reconstruction

IT IS WINTER. NATURE SEEMS dead, but do not be deceived: snowdrops peek out from under the snow, pines are still green, trees sleep as they wait for their rebirth and animals only hibernate before rejoining the outside world and a life full of activities. The Tower is in the likeness of winter: it appears to be attacked, but hope and the motivation to rebuild anew emerge.

In this card nature takes back its rights in the middle of winter. Nothing is ever dead, and sometimes deconstruction is needed for a better reconstruction. At times you need to take up the challenge that presents itself even if it seems impossible. The tower depicted in the card is built on a crag, making it a fortress, but the flames assailing it come from an unexpected or unknown source. This invites you to question the usefulness of your own defensive walls or what you have let enter your life, and the utility of leaving well enough alone. It is also an invitation to rebuild your foundations.

From this reconstruction new, happy, explosive and surprising events will emerge. Give yourself the opportunity to rebuild what has been destroyed. You may need to take destruction into your own hands to start anew on healthy foundations.

Traditional key words: emergence, deliverance, construction, joy, shock, excess, collapse, celebration, dance, divine expression, unblocking, rupture

THE STAR

XVII

Imbolc

KEY WORDS — protection, orientation, germination, feminine power

The Star is a card that calls upon your deep intuition, your guiding star or the beliefs that enable you to move forward. It is also a card of inner construction, a sign that a project is getting underway: the woman pours water from a cup into the wider flow but keeps the content of the second cup for herself. She still protects herself from stepping into the world by remaining perched on land,

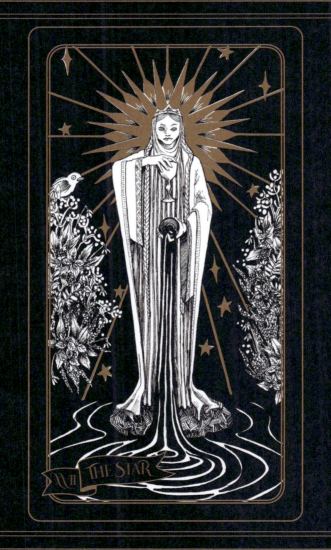

XVII THE STAR

standing in the critical moment between the inner and outer, between spirituality and grounding in the world, between the gestation of her idea and its undertaking. She is surrounded by symbols of Imbolc encouraging her purifying action and her future projects: mistletoe, heather, laurel, basil, snowdrops and rowan.

The Star draws its inspiration from the Imbolc sabbat: the star shining in the night and beaming throughout the card represents the hope that comes with the return of the sun. Light begins to shine in the darkness. Through the purification of water and the ritual with the cups the future is being prepared. You are invited to cleanse, to take a bath to purify yourself, to sort through things and put your projects in order.

The Star can also be interpreted as the power of the feminine, the power of night and hope at the end of the road. She is your lucky star, guiding you in your life and offering you benevolent protection.

Traditional key words: acting in the world, finding your place, sanctifying, fertility, inspiration, femininity, lucky star, cosmos, fluidity

THE MOON

Ostara

gestation, illusion, psychology/ hidden aspect, imagination, darkness

THE MOON CAN HAVE MANY meanings depending on your reading. Rather than being represented in a particular phase the moon is symbolic or multiple, shown in many moments of its cycle for this card is always a sign of evolution, of change, of the fact that nothing is permanent or what it seems to be because you can never know what is hidden on the dark side of the moon or in earth's shadow. Night hides all that goes on during that time, giving a mysterious and intense character to things and sometimes making them as crazy, astonishing and spectacular as a dream. Where is illusion; where is reality? What is hidden in the deep psyche in which you never venture? The Moon can invite you to explore or reveal the answers to these many questions.

The half-immersed figure is like your unconscious, emerging but not quite with you. The figure is passive, and its gaze isn't directed towards you. It just exists and shows itself to you, sometimes voluntarily. Underwater, some shadow areas remain. What is the cause of the bubbles, the leaves and the flowers on the water's apparently peaceful surface? Is what you see reality or is it a reflection of reality?

The rabbits and eggs of Ostara, hidden in the daffodils, lilies and violets, remind you that The Moon is also the card of fertility and gestation, of what grows in you without showing itself. Abundance is showing its first signs without quite yet revealing itself. The Moon can be one of these things or all of them. It is a card of mystery.

Traditional key words: feminine power, night, intuition, dreams, mystery, attraction, imagination, gestation, poetry, uncertainty

XVIII · THE MOON

XVIIII THE SUN

KEY WORDS clarification, emotion, generosity, unconditional love

THE SUN IS A SHINING CARD

in your reading that brings unconditional love and light and the insight you need. As long as the sun god is here you feel protected and warmed. The Sun is the complement of The Moon, that part of your being that is in plain view. It can also be the sign that a hidden element must be revealed.

The Sun's radiance floods everything, including the truth. This card is therefore an invitation to bring things to light, to clarify them or sort through them. The god, father of all beings, is also a symbol of family, paternity and the home. He can be synonymous with a warm, absolute love – not passion, but a protecting and accepting love.

Traditional key words: masculine archetype, construction, warmth, love, new life, construction, brotherhood/sisterhood, shining, childhood, success, evolution, clarification

freedom, recognition, regeneration

JUDGEMENT EMBODIES RESURRECTION, the ultimate step before The World card, before achieving total victory with your head turned towards the sky but your feet still well grounded in the earth. Judgement is a card of movement, of transitioning from darkness to light and from one state to another.

Judgement is a renewal, a birth or recognition finally obtained. It can be a sign of a new stage in your life, a resurrection of the kind you can create as many times as you feel the wish to change and become a better person who is closer to your deep aspirations and values. Here Judgement is represented by a deep and magical realm: ether, the place of all potentialities, the unknown space in the universe where all intentions are formed and realised and where magic acquires and exercises its power. Ether has no beginning and no end; he/she is like the state of meditation and is pure energy. As he/she is sometimes considered to be both the union and the creator of the four other elements then he/she is the fifth element, useful for

the practise of magic. The point is not to understand or see ether but to feel that its existence is already a part of your life as soon as you want it to be.

Traditional key words: new consciousness, desire, vocation, resurrection, rebirth, calling, transcendence, emergence, divine call

XXI THE WORLD

The goddess

KEY WORDS   **victory, completion, the end of a cycle, perfection, self-realisation**

THE WORLD IS THE VICTORIOUS completion of a cycle that unites the elements of the four suits – air, water, fire and earth – around the mandorla containing the victorious figure at the centre of The World. You are reunited with the sorceress in training who left for her spiritual journey in The Fool's card; here she is at the height of her spiritual path. The now-accomplished sorceress has found access to what the non-initiated do not perceive. She feels connected to

THE WORLD

the goddess and has found meaning in her practice, and she knows how to use the elements and deities to put the universe in the service of her intentions and her intentions in the service of the universe. She controls what she gives and what she receives. The goddess protects and guides her, enabling her to feel accomplished and fully mindful of her existence and of the present.

The World marks the end of a happy, victorious cycle, announcing a radiant end and full completion. In the middle or at the beginning of a spread it can symbolise the end of a cycle and therefore a beginning, a return to the starting point that can often be dark and laborious. Everything is to be reinvented in the new cycle about to begin and it is up to the sorceress to send her intention out into the universe.

Traditional key words: resolution, fullness, success, holiness, universality, completion, total victory

THE MINOR ARCANA

Suit of Air

Ace of Air · Fumigation

Key words: new idea, revelation, illumination
Reverse: unkept promises, mental fog, burying your head in the sand

Once your outer space is purified your mind follows the path you showed its environment: fumigation means starting over on solid foundations, giving renewal a chance and re-energising the mind and things. This paves the way for all potentialities stemming from thoughts, ideas and mental clarification. Charged air, on the contrary, can bring a lack of visibility and discernment, a feeling of moving forwards blindfolded.

Key words: indecision, blockage, compromise, being on the threshold of the cavern
Reverse: clarity, obvious decision, good view of the world

Dawn is a metaphor for our being: it highlights our indecision, our first steps into a half-toned situation characterised by hesitation but also by a raw intention waiting to be revealed.

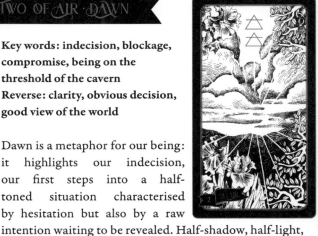

Half-shadow, half-light, dawn can hide a blockage or may need a compromise to express itself. Dawn lacks clarity but it is full of promise.

Key words: first attempts, first thoughts on the world, adolescent attempts to express your ideas
Reverse: fear of revealing yourself, sadness, shyness, adolescent crisis

Hearing, the sense associated with the element of air, is a demand to be heard. It is a call to the world using sound, and it cannot be ignored even if it is sometimes rejected. It's the first step turned outward in your project or idea, hope for the person who calls, good news perhaps or a discovery or feeling of being attacked for the one who receives it.

FOUR OF AIR · BLUE MOON

Key words: rest, time for yourself
Reverse: starting to move,
agitation, anxiety

A blue moon is a second full moon in a calendar month. Here it represents a time out or another opportunity to connect with the goddess, create a ritual, or just contemplate the moon. It is a period of rest, a time for yourself in your bubble or a space of your own.

Key words: dishonesty, treason, brash action
Reverse: being caught red-handed, a way out of a crisis, timorousness

The candles on the altar have melted and mingled, most of them smothering each other. They need to be sorted through to see which ones still shine because all is not dark, although all is not light either: there are positives and negatives in everything. It is up to you to choose whether you want to sink deeper or climb out of the hole. It is up to you to discern who or what is smothering you or betraying your trust.

Key words: leaving a difficult situation, making progress, resisting
Reverse: remaining frozen in place, going back to the starting point

Amethysts promote clarity of thought, balance and serenity and calm the torments of the mind. Represented here as

a raw crystal stone, the amethyst is like a dark cave to explore and traverse in order to reach the light at the end of the tunnel. An amethyst can represent a path of purification or difficult moments. You don't know what happens in the light, but what matters is to walk through your shadows and carve out your own inner crystal.

SEVEN OF AIR · CLOVER

Key words: dishonesty, slyness, concealment
Reverse: fixing a mistake, help, luck

In a patch of clover, a plant of air, it is easy to conceal yourself and try to pass for what you are not. Where are the three-leafed clovers, and where are the four-leafed ones? Are all plants clover? Will you be able to gain an advantage by picking the lucky shoots, or will you feel betrayed and that you are the victim of a false promise?

Key words: self-limitation, feeling paralysed
Reverse: freedom, emancipation

Lavender is associated with protection, purification, renewal and harvest, but it is imprisoned in a sheath preventing it from expressing itself. That sheath, made up of lavender's own branches, symbolises how you limit yourself.

Key words: worry, despair, blocked mind
Reverse: healing, relief, appeasement

The flute is blocked up by lavender imposing its limits on sound, just like the way you can sometimes feel blocked when life should be expressing itself, spilling out and reaching others.

Key words: feeling sick and tired, failure, final hurdle before reaching a higher level in your life
Reverse: starting over from scratch, rebirth, healing

This card usually indicates it is time to move on to something else but that the future or your energy is blocked. Venus invites you to journey, to overcome the limits of your mind in order to venture into the realm of emotion. Connected to the goddess Inanna, this card represents reversing opposites and the order of things that are no longer right for you, going beyond your limits or moving far away from what mentally crushes you.

PAGE OF AIR · IRIS INCENSE

Key words: innovative ideas, intellectual curiosity
Reverse: cowardice, intellectual blockage, blindness

Like ideas, fumigation smoke travels, spreads and reaches the ones it has chosen. Iris, incense of air, is an intellectual booster for those who understand, who capture ideas and

appropriate them then give them value and develop them. But the page is a youthful card, and he might let the opportunity escape him.

QUEEN OF AIR · BARN OWL

Key words: intelligence, logic, eloquence, cutting through, decisions
Reverse: gossip, judgement, lack of discernment, laziness of mind

Tall and majestic, the Queen of Air is wise and proud but also ready to cut through what needs to be decided! She is accompanied by her night animal, the barn owl, and is connected to Athena, the goddess of wisdom, intelligence and eloquence. These qualities may give the impression of a passive card, but the Queen of Air is also gifted with a strong, sharp, lively temperament.

KING OF AIR · FEATHER

**Key words: intelligence,
brightness of mind,
decision-maker
Reverse: pitiless, cutting,
evil tongue**

The King of Air is the symbol
of wisdom, the absolute and
insightful mind. He is able to
rise to the highest heights but
can also lose himself in the
depths of his thinking, thus
dragging you into the darkest
corners of your thoughts – those that aim to hurt others
through ill-intentioned words and reasoning.

Key words: making yourself heard, asserting yourself
Reverse: using words to hurt, taking revenge

The Knight of Air stands under the constellations of his element: Gemini, Libra and Aquarius. These are the constellations of the astrological signs of eloquence, the expression of intellect and mind and of communication. This knight goes off hunting for ideas and finds them, brings them home and even spreads some of his own. He has a tendency towards disorganisation or misusing his eloquence and ideas and his ability to communicate.

SUIT OF WATER

Key words: new love, new momentum, pure emotion
Reverse: emotional blockage, disappointment in love or friendship

In this card the element of water expresses its purest aspect. It pulls everything along with it, for the ace is the card of all potentialities, all hopes. Water gushes down into a wider flow. It is the element of emotion, and so it is in this area that things fall into place and open up for you.

TWO OF WATER · TWILIGHT

Key words: collaboration, friendship, emotional healing
Reverse: separation, toxic relationship

Twilight is an in-between time, a fresh start, darkness and light aligned to create a beautiful moment. It represents your loves and friendships, and the people you feel good with who bring benevolence into your life. These relationships make your life sweet without making you feel invaded by them.

THREE OF WATER · TASTE

Key words: partying, celebration, support
Reverse: solitude, insipidness

Taste is the sense associated with the element of water, and it is a sign of partying, of joyful communal living and of sharing.

Without it your life will seem insipid. To feel the friendship and support expressed by the Three of Water, think of the joy experienced by your taste buds when you feast on delicious foods.

Key words: boredom, stagnation, withdrawal
Reverse: new enthusiasm, opportunity

Like the last quarter moon, the Four of Water is a half-toned card: neither passive nor active, reflected in calm waters free of any waves and disturbances with nothing to unsettle them but nothing to enliven them either. It is a card of balance but not of perfection, so it can reflect a level of boredom or stagnation or simply the fact of being on the sidelines of social life.

FIVE OF WATER · INDIGO CANDLE

Key words: disappointment, regrets, loss, mourning
Reverse: forgiving, moving on

This card seems idyllic with its beautiful, welcoming fireplace yet it invites you to take a step back. The fireplace has been closed off and no fire will ever burn in it again. The candle flames are flickering, sometimes invisible, in the wax hollows that might smother them in the end. The wax starts to run uncontrollably, as if to expel what needs to be eliminated – a time of mourning, of looking back towards the past, of regrets – until the flames are ready to show themselves to the world once more and shine in the eyes of all.

SIX OF WATER · AQUAMARINE

Key words: nostalgia, romanticism, gentleness, contemplation of beauty
Reverse: weight of the past, remorse, regret

The raw aquamarine exacerbates feelings and emotions. It's an unfinished crystal of balance and beauty tending towards the idealisation of the object of your thoughts. Mounted on a ring, the aquamarine is held towards the earth, towards immobility, a foundation that will never reach to a higher level. Its splendour represents your hopes and its foundation the uncertain vapours of your past.

SEVEN OF WATER · THYME

Key words: illusion, emotional overload, temptation
Reverse: emotional clarification, control

When you want to do too much you can muddle your mind. The time has come to clarify things, to distinguish what is true from what is false and to lift the veil of illusion before your eyes.

EIGHT OF WATER · LOTUS

Key words: moving forward, moving on to something else, emotional completeness
Reverse: feeling stuck, despair

The lotus, a flower of transformation, harmony, rebirth and emotions, is surrounded by the mudras of balance, water and purification in perfect symmetry. The Eight of Water is a card of perfect emotional balance but it is also a sign that it's time to move on to something else, to the mind and to the importance of spirituality.

NINE OF WATER · CAULDRON

Key words: emotional comfort, comfort zone
Reverse: letting yourself go, greed, toxic behaviour

The cauldron is a magic tool of spell making and ritual. It is a symbol of success in a particular personal practice in which you feel confident, secure and comfortable. The cauldron represents emotional security within your own magical system or your own comfort zone.

TEN OF WATER · MERCURY

Key words: harmony, happiness, emotional security
Reverse: family tension, rupture, depression

Mercury, the planet closest to the sun, represents a warm, reassuring space such as a hearth. It gives the feeling of being surrounded, of having a rich social life and of being included in sharing.

PAGE OF WATER · ORCHID INCENSE

Key words: temptation in love, new emotion, awakening
Reverse: emotional immaturity, toxic choices

Like the Page of Water, the orchid has virtues that attract love and harmony. Like a blooming flower the Page of Water is still in the hesitation of youth, opening himself up to feelings and love and wondering about himself and about the feelings of others. His senses are heightened.

QUEEN OF WATER · SWAN

Key words: empathy, intuitive sensitivity, protection
Reverse: emotional overload, lunacy, hypersensitivity

Floating on water on the back of a swan, an animal of beauty, emotion, love and intuition, the Queen of Water, gifted with the same qualities as her ride, is the symbol of empathy and pure emotion. Like water she can be limpid, calm and gentle or troubled, opaque and capable of engulfing you. She is fully focused on her intuition and on her sometimes overflowing emotions.

Key words: generosity, confidence, serenity
Reverse: abusive behaviour, manipulation, dishonesty

Like any monarch the King of Water is a figure of abundance – here, of abundant emotion like his element of water. Born of froth, he sits in a cornucopia of abundance overflowing with shells, which are a sign of his empathy, generosity and confidence in the people around him and in his social relationships. The King of Water is a situation or a person you can trust.

Key words: charming prince or princess, romanticism, movement
Reverse: immaturity, jealousy

The Knight of Water stands under the constellations of his element: Pisces, Cancer and Scorpio. He shows you the way, the path towards a gentler place. This path can also be an invitation to face the truth you can sometimes knowingly refuse to see. It is up to you to embrace the best of these zodiac personalities – intuition, imagination and empathy – or their worst: hypersensitivity, chaos and slyness.

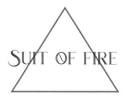

SUIT OF FIRE

ACE OF FIRE · FIRE

Key words: vitality, creative birth, sexual explosion, positive renewal
Reverse: lack of motivation, lack of preparation, sexual blockage

The element of fire expresses the rawest form of energy, of creative force, but also passion or sexual energy. Fire can be an inner fire and can evoke a motivating or consuming influence. It can also be your own vitality as well as your need to express yourself, to reveal what dwells inside you.

Key words: choosing your path, planning, building a project
Reverse: fear of the unknown, inability to find your own path

Noon is the time of day connected to intentions of strength and will and attracting things through force of determination. As the Two of Fire, noon magnifies strong decisions connected to your projects and creations as well as to their planning and, broadly speaking, their development in your mind.

THREE OF FIRE · SIGHT

Key words: expansion, first steps, creative experiments
Reverse: obstacles, limiting yourself

The Three of Fire is the card of first steps, of adolescent life testing that is uncontrolled and full of enthusiasm. Imagine you are observing the world through that first sense of sight, and you suddenly feel a desire to discover everything, to always see more. However, the many eyes in the imagery symbolise that it is up to you to decide what you look at and how you look at it, and that your senses are directed towards the world or towards your interiority. The way you want to explore the world, to invade it with your seeking and diligence, will always be personal and unique.

FOUR OF FIRE · LAST CRESCENT MOON

Key words: harmony, celebration, friendship
Reverse: reserve, close-mindedness, solitude

The waning moon, particularly the last crescent moon, is a good time to start a transformation. Like the moon, nothing is permanent; your life is constantly subject to change. It is the same for all of us, and whatever phases we are in we all go through the same things, walking side by side, paths crossing and meeting and journeying together, and celebrating the moments of sharing and support that form a greater all.

Key words: rivalry, conflict, confrontation, challenge
Reverse: harmony, resolution

As they carry out their functions some candles continue to burn while others have blown out. Some lie on the ground, having lost their usefulness. The Five of Fire asks you about your position in the conflict or confrontation you are experiencing.

SIX OF FIRE · PYRITE

Key words: victory, triumph, recognition, respect, self-confidence in what you undertake
Reverse: selfishness, humiliation, revelation of something negative, lack of self-confidence

The pyrite is a crystal of fire that strengthens concentration, the mind and creativity. It can come in the form of a rock, but when cracked open it looks like gold and shines brightly. Here the pyrite asserts its majestic presence, claiming the praise that is its due. It inspires you with self-confidence and dazzling creativity.

SEVEN OF FIRE · MINT AND PEPPER

Key words: struggling against adversity, defending your point of view, facing up
Reverse: abandonment, lack of motivation, weak thought

Mint and pepper, connected to the element of fire, symbolise the difficulties met throughout life, the simple things that can sometimes become tangled and mixed up, the struggle to be the first to reach your goals while growing or expressing your strength and tastes. The Seven of Fire is a card of powerful expression and adversity.

EIGHT OF FIRE · EUCALYPTUS AND HIBISCUS

Key words: rapid change, speed, travel, perfection of the creative realm
Reverse: brutal stop, backpedalling, creative block

Eucalyptus, which connects the earth and the spiritual world, is used for inspiration, energy and progress and grows ever higher towards the goal to be attained. It seems to stretch in endless lines, to invite you to explore new places, travel, be curious and reach a goal symbolised by the beauty of the hibiscus, a flower of desire and the perfect expression of the fire suit. Represented by blooms reaching their peak, the Eight of Fire is the explosion of your creativity, of your desire or sexual completion. This is the card of ultimate accomplishment, of results obtained before exploring a new area in your life.

NINE OF FIRE · MAGIC WAND

Key words: narrow-mindedness, staying the course, moving forward whatever the cost
Reverse: seeing beyond appearances, opening your mind, moving on to something else

The magic wand can be perceived as an end in and of itself or the ultimate means to attain your goal and give life to your intentions, but it is only an element, a channel, of

the path. Use it to open your mind rather than as the limited and finite expression of your desires. The Nine of Fire also indicates narrow-mindedness or wearing blinkers, or it invites you to see beyond appearances and show some imagination.

TEN OF FIRE · MARS

Key words: responsibilities, seeing red, feeling sick and tired
Reverse: offloading a weight, taking a healthy break

This card is a warning, an invitation to let go and move on to something else. It marks a feeling of being overloaded by tasks or responsibilities, of an excessive emotional or mental charge. You feel overwhelmed and ready to give up in the face of what awaits you. Mars exalts inside you what is just waiting to explode. It's time to look further out, to take a different path.

Key words: creative energy, clumsy enthusiasm, insouciance of youth
Reverse: pessimism, fear of revealing yourself, limiting thoughts

Like any page the Page of Fire is in between two things, is in the middle of hatching. He is the most exalted, ardent and committed of all pages, living on passion and creativity, and has not thought of consequences. He reveals himself fearlessly, all the while retaining the modesty of his youth and fiercely protecting his inner child.

QUEEN OF FIRE · SERPENT

Key words: passion, determination, creativity
Reverse: anger, unkindness, blind vengeance

The Queen of Fire is powerful and determined. She tries to dominate you or her surroundings, looking to model things in her image according to what she thinks. She is a creative source born directly of the power of fire. The tamed serpent that encircles her without oppressing her is the primal energy of life, the connection with the earth. Together they are passion and life force, but they can also smother and kill.

KING OF FIRE · COAL

Key words: determination, control, passion
Reverse: arrogance, contempt, theatricality

The King of Fire is a card of creative power, of confidence in the ability to create the world from scratch and of ardent expression to galvanise crowds. He can seem limitless, as if he was made only of his inner fire and evocative energy. In the middle of this all-consuming passion, however, he can also be arrogant, contemptuous, full of self-importance and aware of his capacity to move mountains.

Key words: passion, desire, motivation, dynamism, adventure, daring, putting yourself in the spotlight
Reverse: badly channelled energy, bad result, libido problems, much ado about nothing

The Knight of Fire stands under the constellations of his element: Aries, Leo and Sagittarius. He is the one who motivates you to join with your desires, your passions, that fire burning inside you that is just waiting to be expressed. He drives you to move towards other horizons, to act, travel and listen to or find your motivation. He brings your truth out of the depths of your being. Sometimes he can make a lot of fuss for nothing; it depends on whether you decide to get up on the horse and move or whether you prefer to stay where you are.

SUIT OF EARTH

ACE OF EARTH · PLANTS

Key words: financial opportunity, hope of abundance, health
Reverse: weakness, greed, preconceived notions on abundance

Earth is the ultimate symbol of all potentialities: it gives birth to all beings and brings forth majestic trees and plants and flowers of immeasurable beauty and virtues from the simple seeds you plant. Earth is the source of life, of growth and expansion. Like an echo, the Ace of Earth reflects abundance, blossoming, growth and, more specifically, material opportunities.

Key words: balance of resources, doing your best, needing a helping hand
Reverse: imbalance, feeling overwhelmed, laziness

Night is the time of day associated with the element of earth and the time of unexpectedness and rebalancing. It is the darkness in which you don't necessarily see things coming. The Two of Earth is the card of balancing material resources, of trial and error and of doing your best but easily feeling overwhelmed, of feeling you are in over your head without understanding why.

THREE OF EARTH · TOUCH

Key words: collaboration, team spirit, clumsy enthusiasm
Reverse: fixing the mistakes of others, intrigue, rejecting help

Touch, the sense associated with the element of earth, shows that you can become multiple using only one sense. Touch is experienced through the entire body and with it you encounter other bodies, other forms of matter or another life that completes you. The Three of Earth reflects this multiplying effect of thought and knowledge through contact and collaboration.

FOUR OF EARTH
WAXING GIBBOUS MOON

**Key words: retention, not seeing past the end of your nose, preserving what has been gained
Reverse: letting go, making projections, showing generosity**

Although it looks like it, the moon is not yet quite full. A waxing gibbous moon is the lunar phase conducive to attracting things, making requests to the universe and searching for abundance among other things. You have finished planning your ascent, and

the Four of Earth is a time of retention before you give yourself to the world and embark on your path towards complete balance, abundance and prosperity. This card marks a fear of letting go of what has been gained, a fear of looking at what lies further ahead and of moving out of your comfort zone.

FIVE OF EARTH · GOLDEN CANDLE

Key words: clumsy or negative movement towards prosperity, putting all your eggs in one basket, forced frugality
Reverse: stability, end of difficulties

The Five of Earth is a sign of loss, of a time of poverty or frugality in your material or physical life. It is symbolised by a single candle whose flame struggles to shine at the top of an altar that is artificially elevated but devoid of intention and other tools, perhaps due to a lack of possibilities. Its base should be strengthened.

SIX OF EARTH · MALACHITE

Key words: sharing, giving, expansion
Reverse: avarice, lack of sharing, selfishness

The malachite mandala expresses two things: harmony through its form and repetition, and expansion through its crystals turned outwards like the rays of the sun. Malachite is a crystal of sharing, prosperity, abundance and giving. The Six of Earth represents that sharing, that expansion; it is turned towards others and their material, tangible experience.

SEVEN OF EARTH · SAGE

Key words: effort, labour, discipline
Reverse: laziness, bad investment

Sage, which is commonly used for purification and in magic rituals, requires time and patience in its preparation. It grows in the garden and must be cut fresh, then it must be dried and carefully rolled into a smoke stick. It can spread its benefits through the smoke it makes when burned. The Seven of Earth represents the time, patience and care given to sage. Things don't happen on their own or with the help of other people when you want them to be done in the way you'd like.

EIGHT OF EARTH · HONEYSUCKLE

Key words: productivity, work, skill
Reverse: loss of motivation, frustration, giving up

All work pays off, like seeds of honeysuckle growing and blooming into the plant that symbolises learning, money, skills and prosperity. This card can indicate a period of work that brings results or the results themselves and what you do with them.

NINE OF EARTH · PENTACLE

Key words: security, abundance, full health
Reverse: fear of losing everything, fear of being on the losing side

The Nine of Earth is a card of abundance, good health and material results. It is represented by a pentacle made by the sorceress according to an accomplished ritual of her own creation, surrounded by her personal tools. She has come to understand her needs and desires in her magic rituals and has built her own universe around her, her own protective world in which she feels safe.

TEN OF EARTH · EARTH

Key words: possessions, transmission, next step
Reverse: squander, waste, grounded in the past

Earth, the planet of grounding and home, symbolises the element of earth's completion: planet Earth whole, global, reflecting both Gaia and Isis, ready for harvest and ready for your own harvest. Not only is the Ten of

Earth a card of prosperity, it also goes beyond that abundance because it enables transmission, affirms the finality of what you have built and can even reveal your full health. Well grounded in the earth, your mind is ready to elevate itself and recognise other considerations such as spirituality and mental work, which can then finally enter into your life. However, abundance can attract accumulation and pollution into your life, preventing you from recognising what truly matters to you.

PAGE OF EARTH · JASMINE INCENSE

Key words: new project, desire to take the plunge, hesitation to undertake something
Reverse: disappointment in finances, beginner, lack of determination

The Page of Earth focuses all his attention on a jasmine shoot, not realising that jasmine as a whole is already coming to him, blooming and blossoming and spreading through its incense smoke. The Page of Earth

has this youthful naivety of seeing the world only through a narrow lens that he believes is the truth. He is just waiting to open himself to the world to discover its riches, undertake new projects and exist.

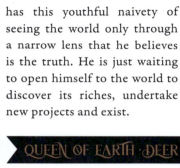

QUEEN OF EARTH · DEER

Key words: centred on the home, materialistic, looking for comfort and security
Reverse: home/work or inner/ outer imbalance, fear of change

Like any queen the Queen of Earth is grounded in her element, almost blending in with it. The deer is an animal of majesty, of earth and of the forest, attracting abundance and knowledge. The Queen of Earth is grounded in her home, in material comfort that she is not ready to give up. She is the manager, the accountant and the builder. She is the mother, the one who occupies the inner home hidden from the world. She can also cling to her comfort zone, resisting change that can sometimes come into her life even if it represents an opportunity.

KING OF EARTH · OAK

Key words: abundance, ostentatious wealth, power
Reverse: hold on others, authoritarian attitude, avarice

The King of Earth is a card of abundance in all that this can represent in terms of power, ostentatious wealth and sometimes contempt towards others. The King of Earth's wealth can cut him off from the rest of the world, but it can also drive him to great generosity. He is grounded in his element but he can already see further out beyond his own limits. He is the one who undertakes and sets up what is needed in order to build what he has imagined. The material world is not a limit.

Key words: practicality, methodical mind, movement
Reverse: immaturity, stubbornness

The Knight of Earth stands under the constellations of his element: Taurus, Virgo and Capricorn. He is a figure of ruthless, methodical logic who invites you to plan, to organise; he dislikes leaving any room for improvisation. He can also call you to order or ask you to show greater flexibility. He sees things through to their end and stops at nothing. Although he is quite stubborn, he can demonstrate stability, perseverance and calm but he can also be down in the dumps, contemptuous and resistant to change and a perfectionist.

ACKNOWLEDGEMENTS

I WOULD LIKE TO THANK LE LOTUS et l'Éléphant as well as my editor, Séverine Corson-Schneider, for giving me the opportunity to write and illustrate this tarot with complete freedom of expression and for unquestioningly letting me use inclusive writing in this booklet, thereby allowing me to create this tarot in absolute keeping with my values.

ABOUT THE AUTHOR

Bérengère Demoncy has exercised her expertise in everything from publishing to fashion and the creation of illustrated card decks. For a number of years she has been the creative director behind Gastronogeek, mixing cuisine and pop culture and restoring the aura of fabulous grimoires. Her current work is inspired by pop culture and the esoteric world of tarot, which she designs and practises with love and intuition.

Learn more about Bérengère Demoncy's work on social media at beren_illustree.